Claude Debussy

THREE GREAT ORCHESTRAL WORKS

In Full Score

Prélude à l'après-midi d'un faune

Nocturnes

La Mer

Dover Publications, Inc., New York

This Dover edition, first published in 1983, is a new one-volume edition of three separate works reproduced from early French editions (see Contents for further bibliographical data): *Prélude à l'après-midi d'un faune*, *Nocturnes* and *La Mer*. The Contents and the Glossary of French Terms are new features of the present edition.

Library of Congress Cataloging in Publication Data

Debussy, Claude, 1862–1918.
[Orchestral music. Selections]
Three great orchestral works.

The 1st and 3rd works are symphonic poems; the 2nd is a suite.
Contents: Prélude à l'après-midi d'un faune—Nocturnes—La mer.
1. Symphonic poems—Scores. 2. Suites (Orchestra)—Scores.
M1000.D4T5   1983   82-19881
ISBN-13: 978-0-486-24441-9
ISBN-10: 0-486-24441-5

Manufactured in the United States by LSC Communications
24441520   2018
www.doverpublications.com

Contents

Glossary of French Terms

accordez (sur): tune (to)
alto: viola
animé, animez: vivaciously
archet: bow
assez: quite
au mouvement: a tempo; back in (previous) tempo
autres: others
avec: with
à vide: open string
baguette de timb(ale): kettledrum stick
b(ass)on: bassoon
beaucoup: much
bouché, bouchez: with stopping
bouche fermée: sung with mouth closed
calme: calm
cédez: slacken
changez en: change to
chaque: each, every
chevalet: bridge (of string instrument)
cl(arinette): clarinet
contrebasse: double bass
cor angl(ais): English horn
cor (à pistons): (valve) horn, French horn
cuivré, cuivrez: with a forced, hard tone
cymb(ales): cymbals
cymb(ales) ant(iques): "ancient" cymbals, a special form of the instrument
dans: in
de plus en plus sonore et en serrant le mouvement: with more and more volume, while quickening the tempo
divisés (en; par): divisi; divided (into; by)
do: the note C
doux: softly
dureté: harshness
du talon: with the nut of the bow
en animant (surtout dans l'expression): becoming livelier (especially in expressiveness)

en augmentant: crescendo
encore plus: even more
en croisant: crossing the hands
en dehors: prominently
enlever: remove
en retenant: holding back
en s'éloignant davantage: growing more distant
en serrant: stringendo, speeding up
entrée: entrance
et: and
expressif: expressive
fin: end
fl(ûte): flute
gracieux: graceful
g(ran)de fl(ûte): flute
gr(osse)-c(aisse): bass drum
harpe: harp
hautb(ois): oboe
initial: initial, of the beginning
jusqu'à: up to
la: the note A
langueur: languor
léger, légèrement: lightly
lent: slow
lenteur: slowness
lointain: far away, distant
mailloche: mallet, stick
mais: but
marqué: marcato
même: same
mesure: measure
mettez: put (on)
mi: the note E
modéré: moderate
mouv(emen)t (du début): tempo (of the opening)
mouvementé: agitato
naturel: natural, normal
ôtez: remove

ou: or
part(ie): part
pendant: during
p(eti)te fl(ûte): piccolo
peu à peu (animé pour arriver à): gradually (livelier in order to reach)
plus (de): more
pointe: tip
pos(ition) nat(urelle) [OR: *ordinaire*]: normal position
préparez le ton de: prepare the key of
près de: near
presque: almost
pupitre: desk
ré: the note D
reprenez: resume, go back to
retardez: slow down
revenir progressivement au I°. tempo: return gradually to the first tempo
rythme: rhythm
rythmé: rhythmically
sans: without
sec: drily
serrez: speed up, stringendo

seulement: only
si: the note B
sol: the note G
sonore: resoundingly, with volume
souple: supple
sourdine: mute
soutenu: sostenuto
sur: on
tamb(our) m(ilitaire): snare drum
tam-tam: gong
timb(ale): kettledrum
touche: fingerboard
toujours: always
tous: all
très: very
tromp(ette à pistons): (valve) trumpet
tumultueux: tumultuous(ly)
uni(e)s: all together; no longer divisi
un peu (plus): a little (more)
vibrant: vibrating
v(iol)on: violin
v(iolonc)elle: cello
vite: quickly

Prélude à l'après-midi d'un faune

Nocturnes

N° I._Nuages

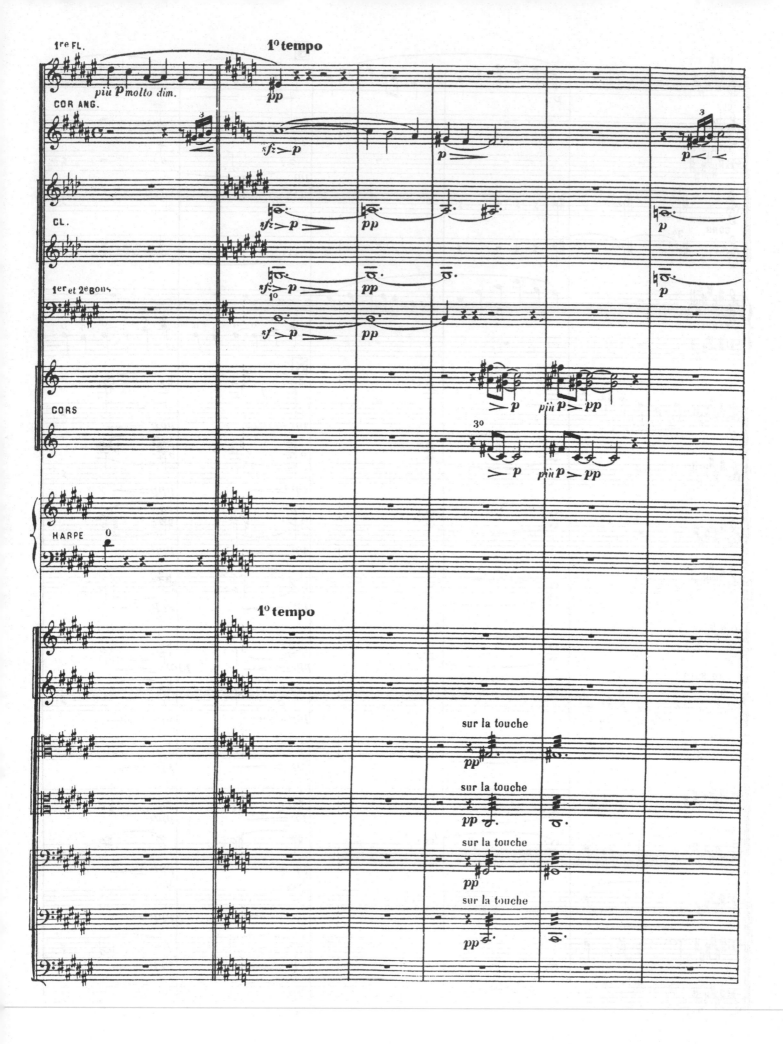

Nº II._ Fêtes

49

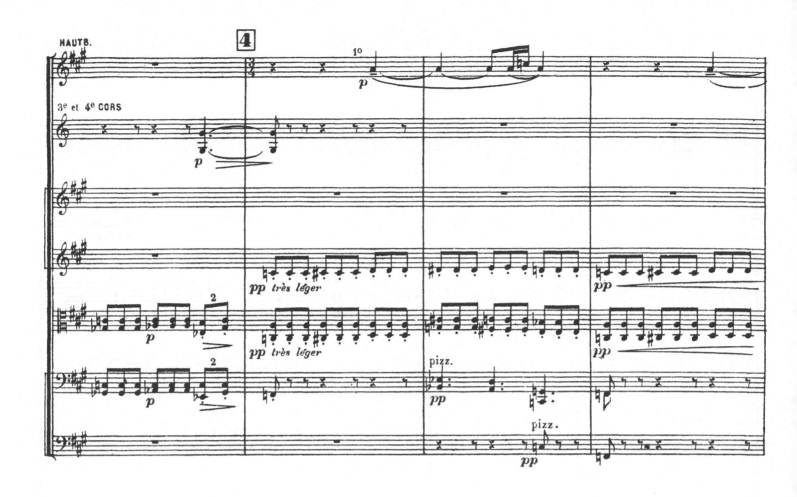

un peu rapproché

Nº III.— Sirènes

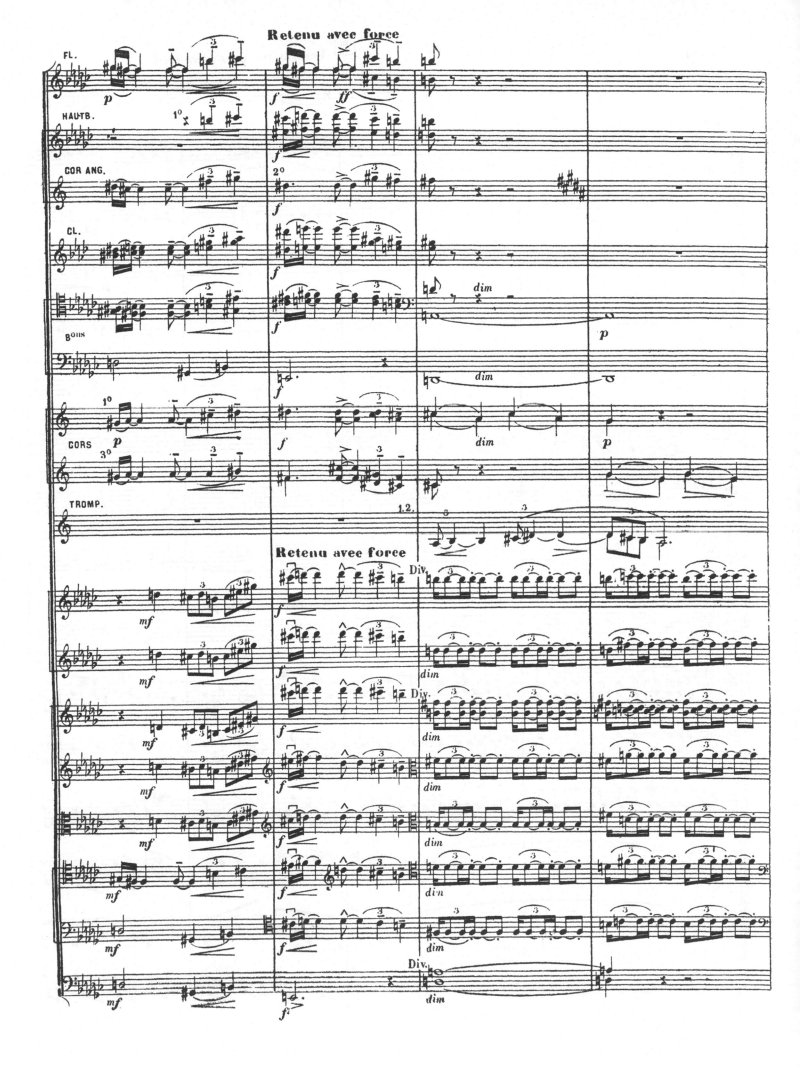

La Mer

I.– De l'aube à midi sur la mer

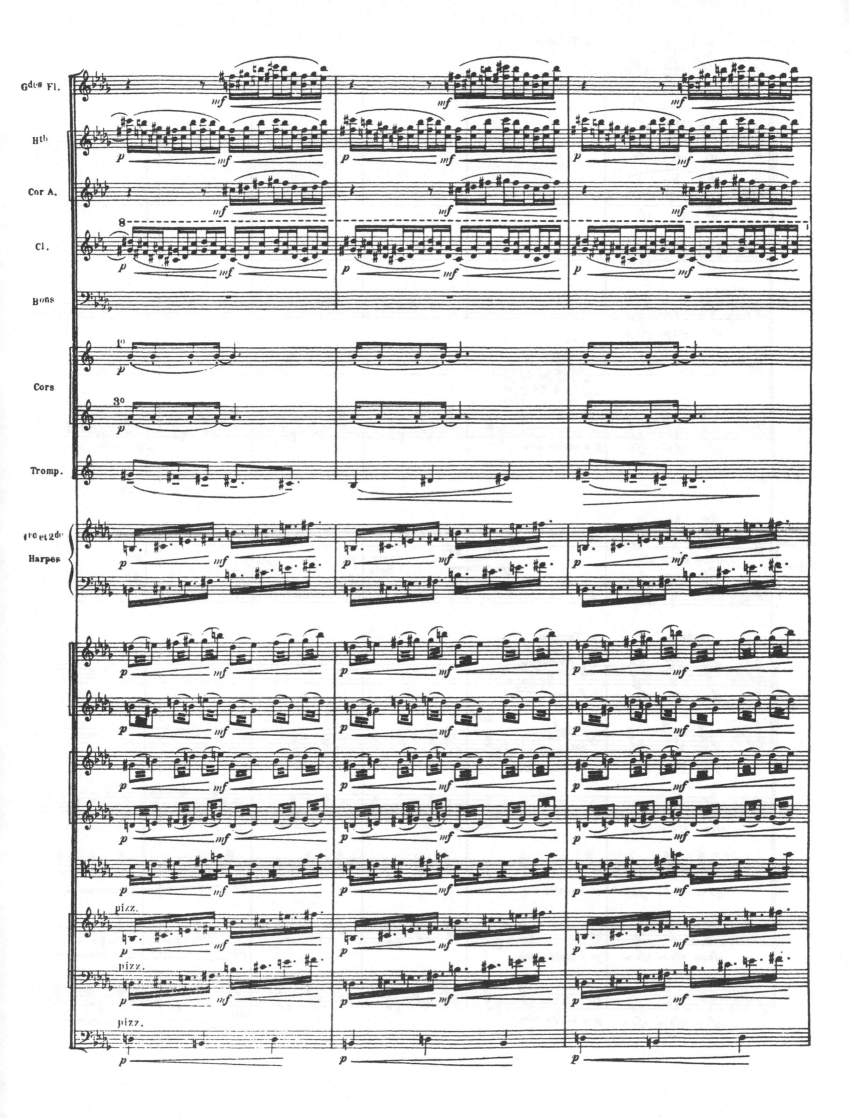

II._ Jeux de vagues

En animant beaucoup

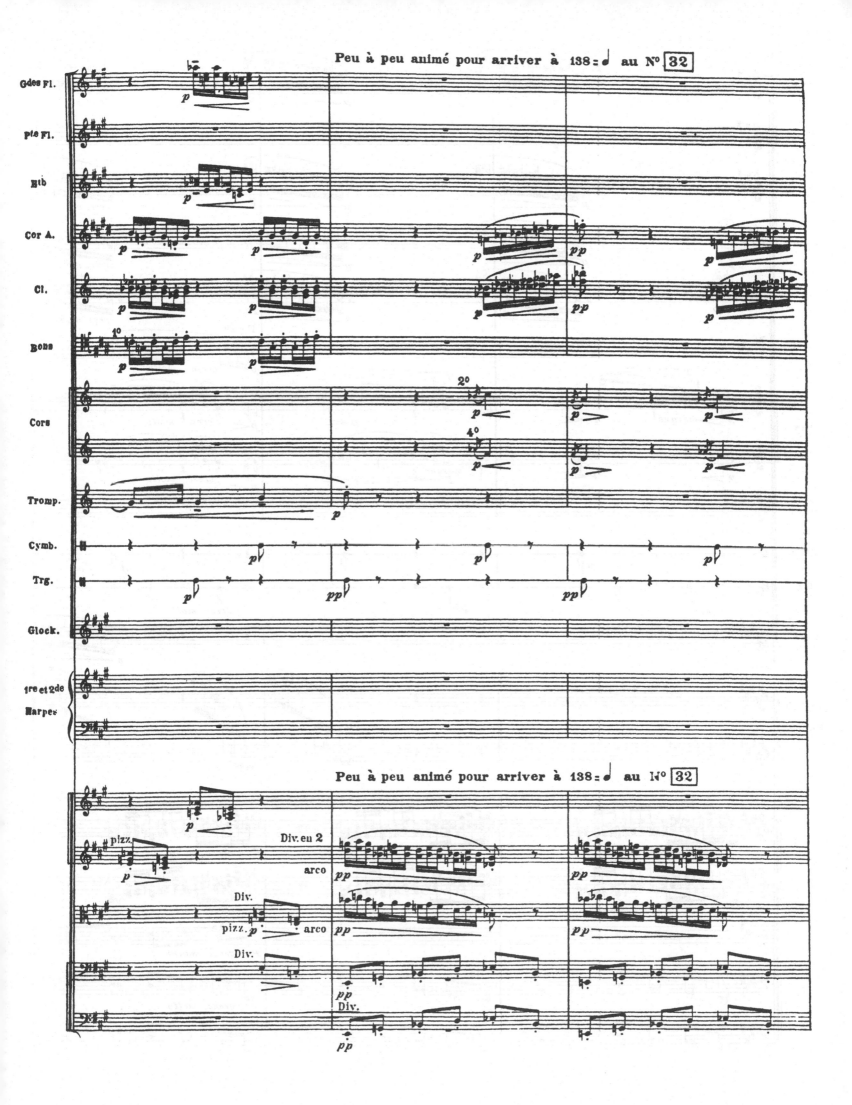

III._ Dialogue du vent et de la mer

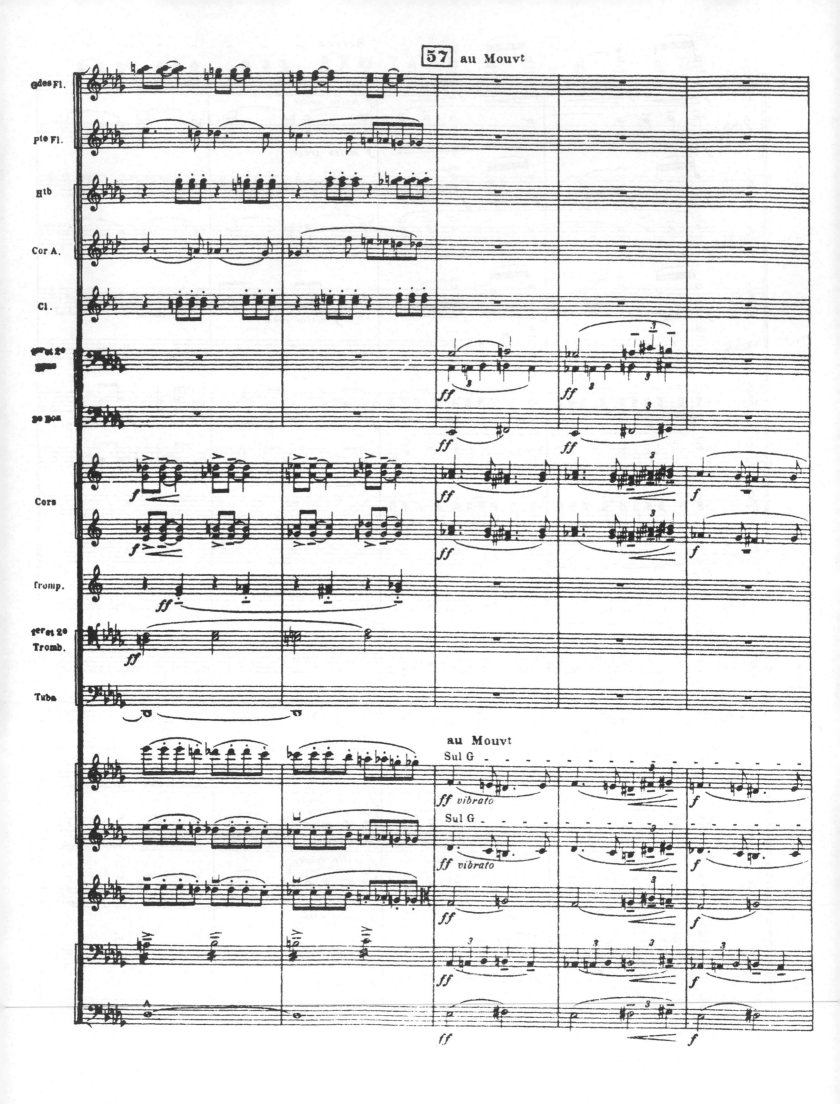

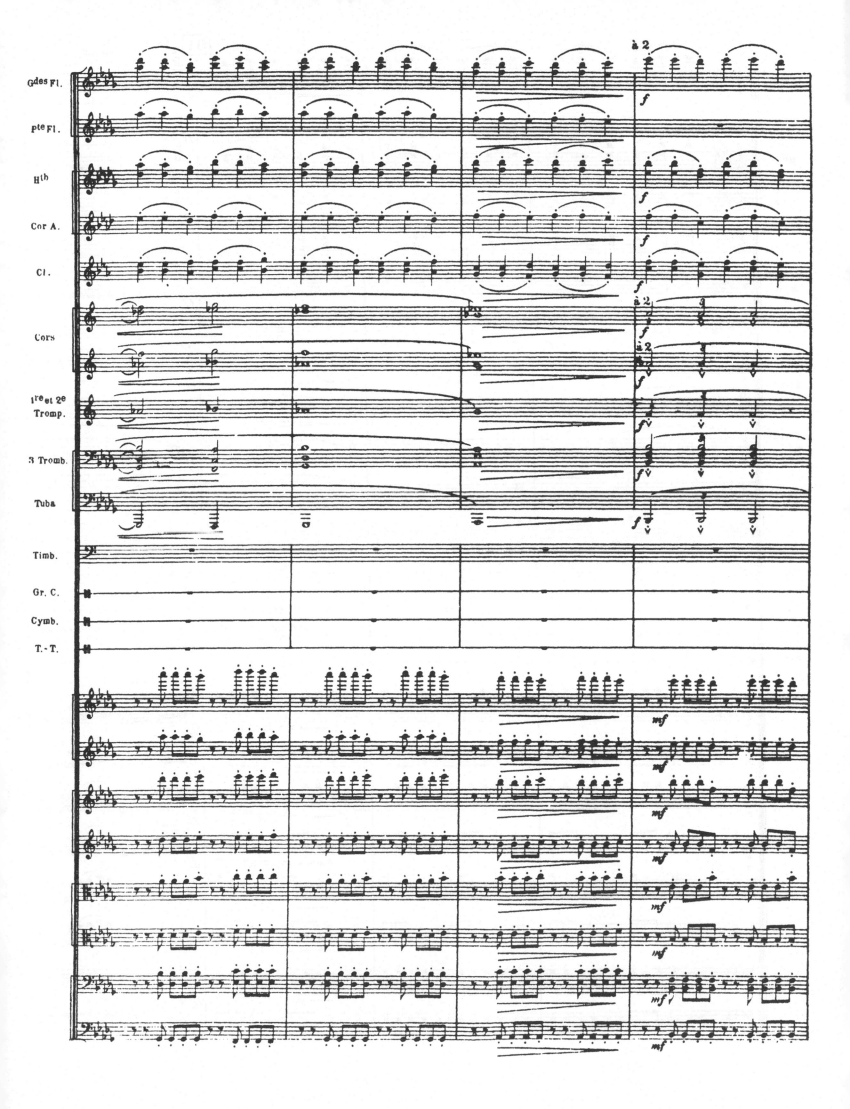